Asu
the Rock Cutter

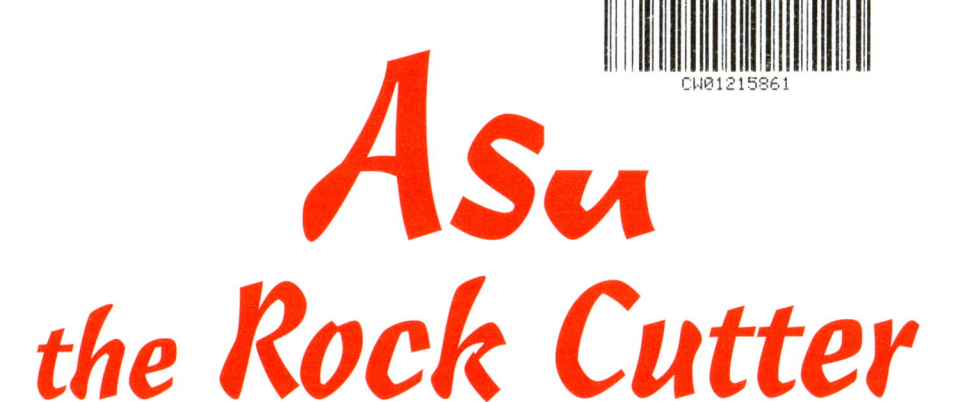

Written by Mio Debnam
Illustrated by Cosei Kawa

Collins

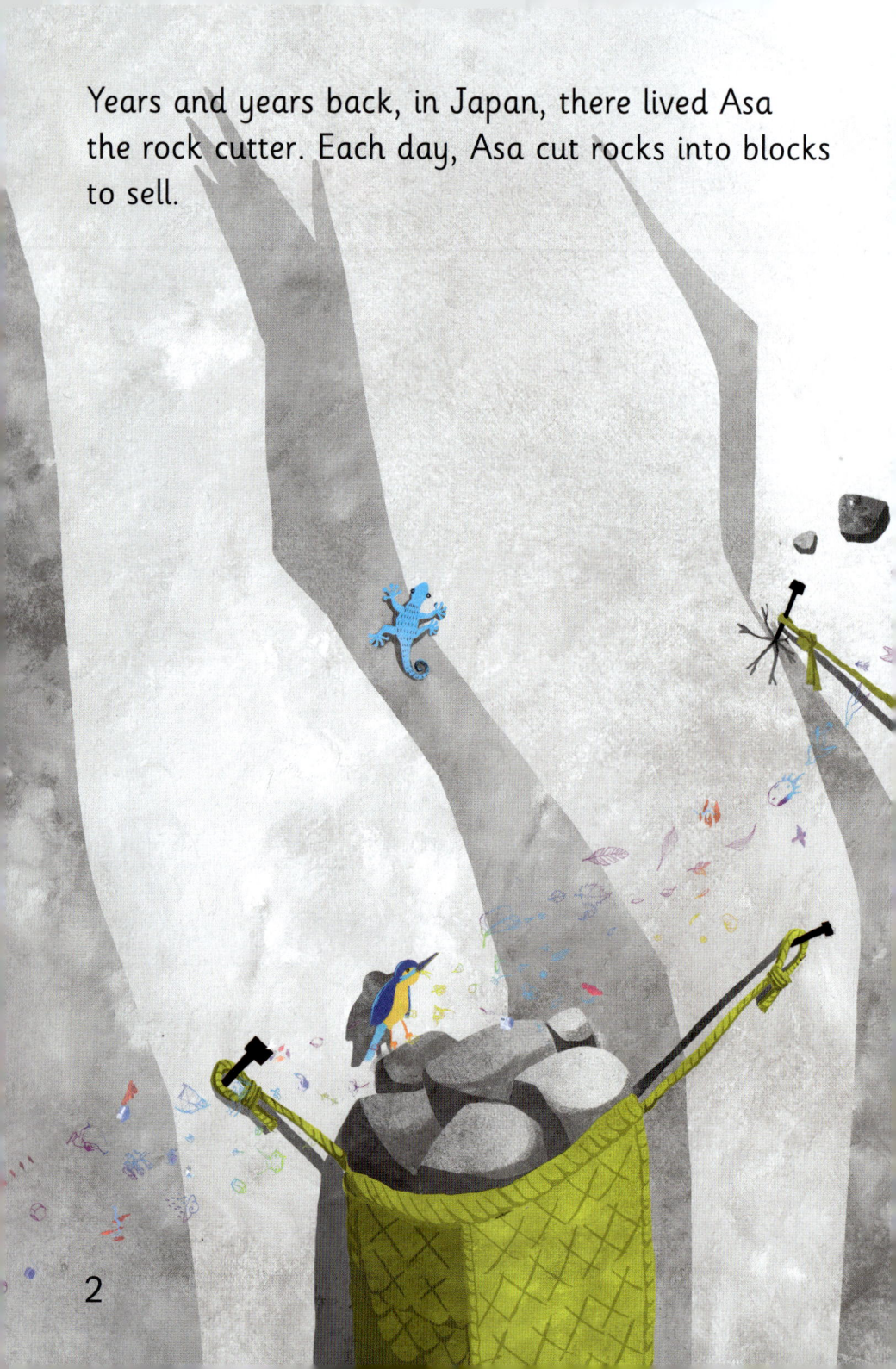

Years and years back, in Japan, there lived Asa the rock cutter. Each day, Asa cut rocks into blocks to sell.

Asa found it hard and he complained.

One day Asa said out loud, "I wish I were rich!"

Swoosh! All of a sudden, he was rich!

Asa was pleased and proud ... for a bit. But that year, the summer was hot. Asa drooped in the heat.

One day he spotted a man with a servant keeping him cool.

"I wish to have a servant too!" cried Asa.

Swoosh! His wish had come true – a servant was fanning him. Asa clapped with joy.

Asa was pleased and proud … for a bit.

But the sun beamed brightly and he was too hot. It dried up streams and scorched the ground.

"The sun is so strong!" he cried.

"I wish I were the sun!" shouted Asa.

Swoosh! All of a sudden, he was the sun, with blue skies all around.

Asa was pleased and proud ... for a bit. But then he spied storm clouds approaching.

To his dismay, the clouds swirled and streaked across the skies.

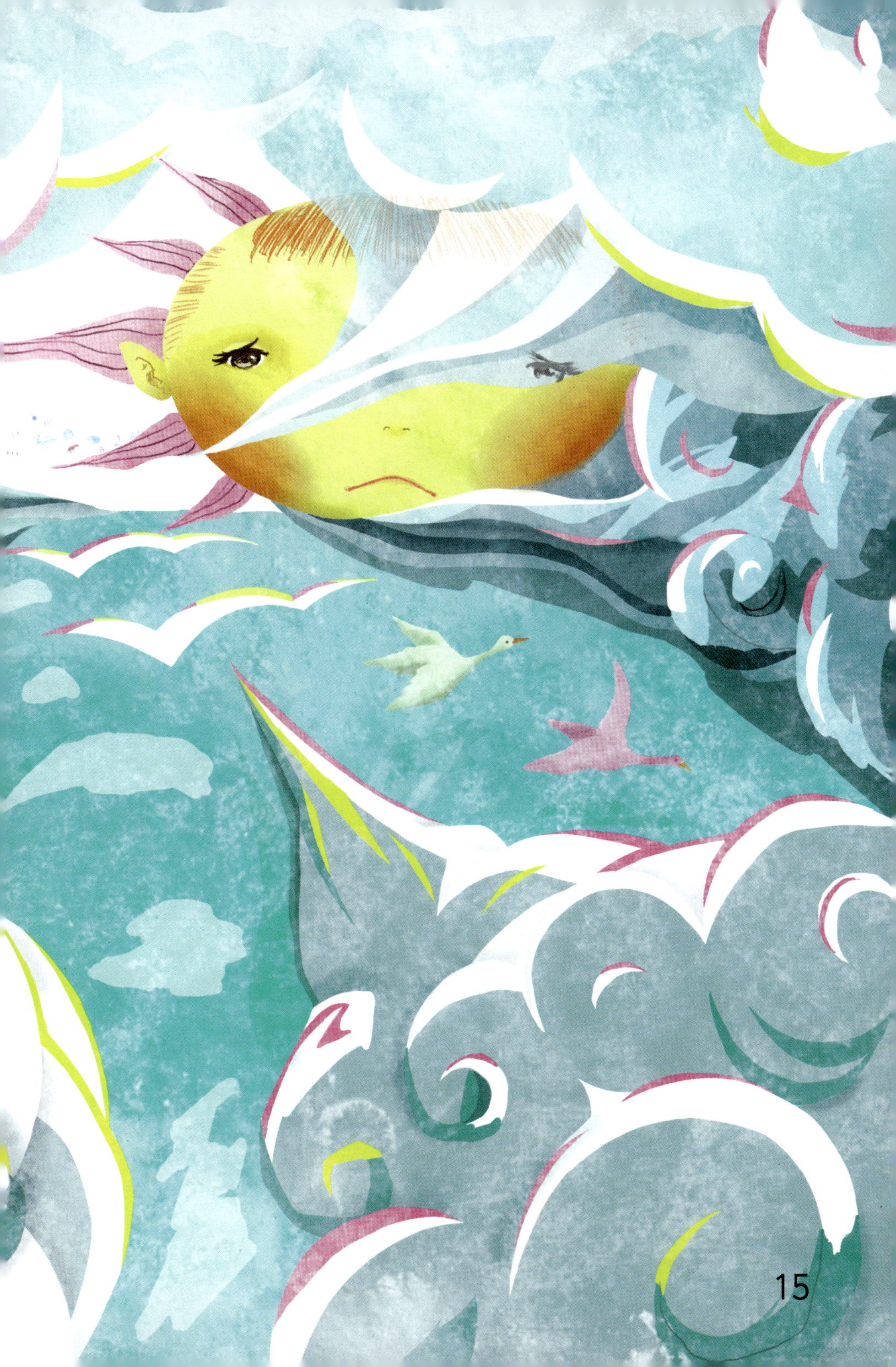

"The clouds have blocked my rays," groaned Asa. "They are stronger than the sun. I wish I were a cloud!"

Swoosh! All of a sudden, he was a cloud!

Asa sent rain beating down. Dams burst and there was mayhem. Men shouted and children cried.

But the rocks on the hills stayed hard and still.

"Rocks are stronger than the clouds and rain! I wish I were a rock!" wailed Asa.

Swoosh! All of a sudden, Asa was a rock. But then he reflected back on the years he had spent cutting up rocks.

"Humans are stronger than rocks!" he cried. "When I was a man, I was stupid. I didn't see my true value. I wish I were a man."

Swoosh! Asa found he was a rock cutter, and he was pleased.

Japan on the map

When it's day in the UK, it's night in Japan.

Japan

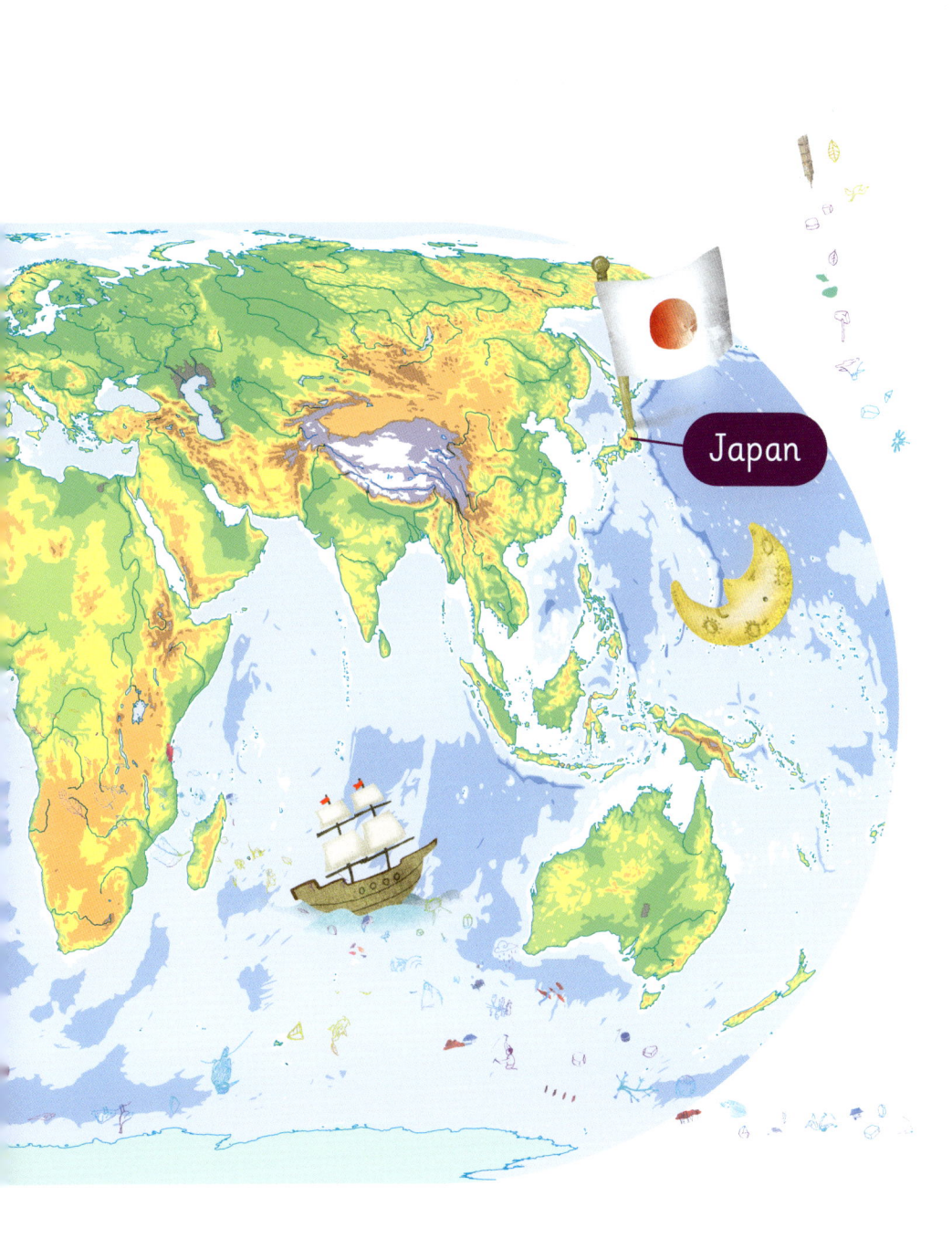

Asa

In Japan, "asa" means "morning".

But the greeting "good morning" sounds like "o-ha-yo".

O-ha-yo!
おはよう

Three things from Japan
Flag
The flag of Japan has the sun on it!

Manga

In Japan, children and adults read manga!

Green tea

Green tea is drunk with meals, with sweet things, or by itself!

Asa

31

🐾 Review: After reading 🐾

Use your assessment from hearing the children read to choose any GPCs, words or tricky words that need additional practice.

Read 1: Decoding
- Turn to pages 10 and 11. Ask: Can you find words that contain each of these sounds: /ee/ and /igh/? How are the sounds spelled? (**pleased**, **beamed**, **streams** – ea; **brightly**, **dried**, **cried** – igh, ie)
  - Repeat for /ow/ and /oo/ on pages 12 and 13. (**shouted**, **around** – ou; **Swoosh**, **blue** – oo, ue)
- Ask the children to read page 8 as fluently as possible. Say: Can you blend in your head when you read the words?

Read 2: Prosody
- Turn to pages 10 and 11.
  - Model reading page 10, pausing at the ellipsis. Discuss how it builds tension.
  - On page 11, discuss the use of the exclamation mark to show Asa's annoyance.
  - Ask the children to read the pages with expression, using the punctuation to build tension.
- Bonus content: Challenge the children to read pages 28 and 29 as if they are a presenter for a travel programme. Remind them to use different tones to add interest and hold the listeners' attention.

Read 3: Comprehension
- Look at the back cover and point to the words **A Japanese tale**. Discuss the meaning of the word **tale** and ask the children what other stories they've read that are based on traditional tales.
- Read the back cover blurb and talk about Asa's wish. Discuss how wishes often occur in stories. Ask: Do characters who get what they wish for usually feel happier? Why, or why not?
- Point to the phrase **true value** on page 22. Say, for example: I would say the true value of this pencil is 15 pence. Ask: Is the phrase used in the same way in the story? What does it mean? (e.g. *real worth – Asa's worth as a human*)
- Look together at the pictures on pages 30 and 31. Encourage the children to use the pictures to help them retell the story in sequence. Can they explain how Asa felt at each stage, and why?
- Bonus content: On page 26, ask the children to practise saying "good morning" in Japanese. Children who know how to say "good morning" in other languages could teach these greetings to the group.